UNREMEMBER

Joel Auterson

Unremember

Published by Bad Betty Press
www.badbettypress.com

Cover design by Joel Auterson

Printed and bound in the United Kingdom

A CIP record of this book is available from the British Library.

ISBN: 978-1-9997147-0-3

UNREMEMBER

To Sarah, for pushing me out of the plane.

And to Chris, for the flying lessons.

Joel Auterson is a poet from Belfast, living in London. He co-hosts Boomerang Club, one of London's best-loved poetry nights, which recently celebrated its third birthday. He's performed around the UK and at festivals like Bestival, Nozstock and the Edinburgh Fringe. He was part of the Roundhouse Poetry Collective in 2014, and was a resident artist at the Roundhouse for two years.

Joel is also a game designer, and runs a tiny studio called Bearwaves. This is his first book.

Contents

For Adam

The sun sleeps
in the dirt, here.
I am less smoke, more steam,
the refreshing kind of bitter.

In the dirt, here,
we'll plant our feet and leave.
The refreshing kind of bitter
lives in my coffee now.

We'll plant our feet and leave.
A tiny, smiling Death
lives in my coffee now.
I am still here, still now.

A tiny, smiling Death,
the sun sleeps.
I am still here, still now;
I am less smoke, more steam.

clunk #1

To deconstruct the lighthouse, then remember why you put it there.

I, protagonist, cried in posh coffee
shop. When we fall apart, we
might as well ensure that the
shapes are beautiful; I could not
help thinking this would make a
poem. Have I? I have too little
lung–no–too much stomach–no–
the knowledge that I can love? I
don't know how much time a rain-
cloud takes to rebuild itself from
an unlit sea. I left about two fifty
and a load of damp napkins. I
have not cried since.

Unremember

When you are born, you come not with an inland sea of
misunderstandings but your own private mythology.

You have words for sky and sea and being that you will
never tell anyone.
                    Over time, you call it *learning*
and you forget this.

When you are five, your knowledge of death comes half
from the Bible and half from the first episode of Pokémon.

Death is different music, heaven is near lapland
is near the moon
and you are, unquestionably, going there.

You know that to grow older is to run to death for a hug
and that this is fine.
                    Over time, you call it *aging*
and you forget this.

When you are twelve, you encounter your first ending that
cannot be resolved by a Pokémon Centre.

You huddle in a suit you don't and a tie you didn't and listen
to a man you will never see again talk about dust and boats.

You learn that the world has ended, and that parents are
not invincible.
            Over time, you call it *healing*
and you forget this.

When you are eighteen, you are the ruler of your own
heart rate, death is a club
you do not have a wristband for and the night has never
had so many colours.

As the city finishes inhaling, a girl will ask for your number
in an empty nightclub and you will wait days for a text.

You have both read the manual and you know how futures
work.
            Over time, you call it *experience*
and you forget this.

When you are twenty, London is an inverted leopard, and
you spend as much time as you can in the bright spots.
When you go home you share a mattress with your
eighteen-year-old self and feel increasingly unwelcome.

It takes you months to realise that the river is at the end
of your street;
            when you do, the cradle tips
and you can hear seagulls again.

You know that there is no romance in curtains that are

never opened.

Over time, you call it *recovery*

and you forget this.

When you are twenty-two, a man called Mike shows up
at the house and
installs an earthquake
between each of your father's knuckles.
You do not ask to see the bill.

You learn that there is nothing so terrifying as the word
palliative.

All at once, and quite deliberately,

you forget this.

clunk #2

Is this too much? / This is too much.

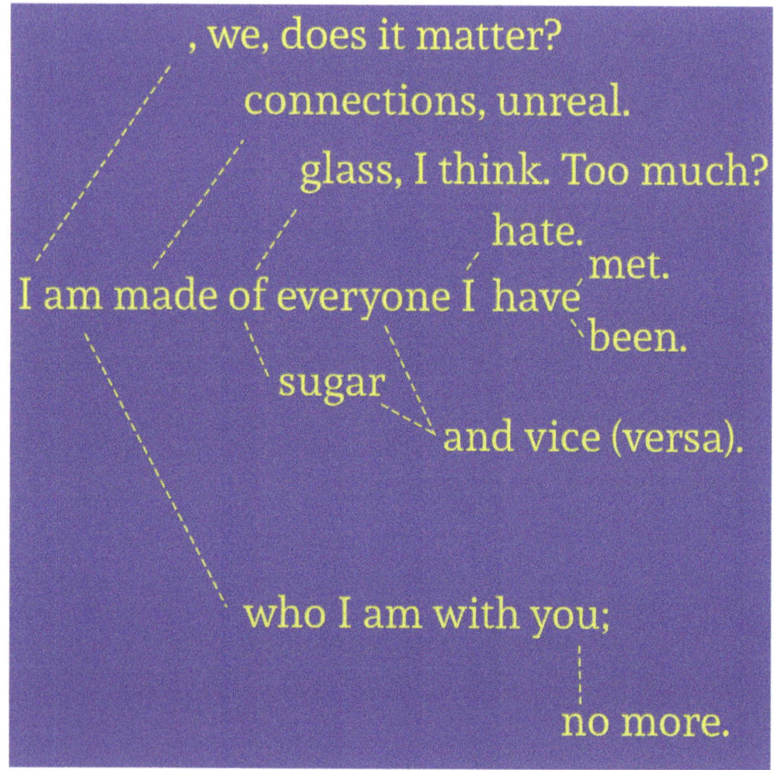

Counting Days

One,
two,
three,
four,
five,
six…

He pauses, eyes closed, face contorted. All of six
years old, his elder siblings have won
spelling bees but he, the youngest of five,
prefers chasing wasps with a stick. Far too
young to appreciate the subtleties or reasons for
mathematics, he simply uses 'lots!' for any number greater than three.

If you ask him, he'll tell you there are only three
facts in this world worth knowing. Six
-ty five million years ago, there were dinosaurs. Some animals have four
feet, some have two, but a snail has only one.
The peregrine falcon has a top speed of over two
hundred miles per hour. He's known that since he was five.

When he gets home from school, he watches TV until five.
"What did you learn today?" He tells Mum what he and three
friends built in the sand. She tries to smile, knowing he'll grow

up all too
soon. This house has more echoes now. Dad works till six
but often doesn't get home till one.
Mum sits near telephones and won't tell the kids what she's
crying for.

The men of the house dig the garden, for
buried treasure and burying secrets. The youngest is five
centimetres down, sure he'll strike dinosaur or at least China one
of these days. His dad used to plant roses in three
neat rows; now he grows turnips. The thorny hedge is six
feet high, but there's a hole: the neighbours grow turnips too.

The washing machine spins at over two
thousand revolutions per minute. He watches for
a while, amazed that he can't even see the clothes. At six
-ty decibels, he can't even hear the shouting. The phone rings five
times, and then cuts out. Mum finds him three
hours later, finger-racing the evening sunlight. Three, two, one...

The next day, he goes to the school library till five,
reads four books, and learns something new in number three.
There were dinosaurs sixty-five million years ago—but the
meteorite won.

clunk #3

Anxiety hymns.

Give me a week to
remember whose ears
heard the last idiotic
thing I said. Just as well
I hid my laugh behind
before the sky folds again.
I'm not entirely confident
of anything, really.
the gallery is still open.
don't look don't look
don't know that
God's favourite frames
(remember the glasses?)
are the ones made from
— fish-hooks
are made to attach
— fists
to what are remembered
as
— friends.
We labour under the sky
(all of us?)
What if there is no
speech to be made?
No applause to take?
What if the horizon is
grey, on and on and
and it goes on and on and on
on and on and on and on and

Sweet Tin

I knew a God once who kept the whole of the sky
in a sweet tin on the windowsill,
beside an armchair that would prove a greater memorial
than any tombstone could. He'd ask it questions like,
"Where is the wind *going*?"
"How do *sheep* become *clouds*?"
"Why do we need *carpets* if we have *grass*?"
"What is the word for 'the smell after the rain stops'?"
I never did find out what the answers were.

This God had a son, and one year he trapped the sun
in a petrol canister, fed it to his motorbike
and launched an assault on roads, mountains and clouds.
He never quite lost the helmet lines—
or the grin.

The God of Earth and Sky would have hated the name.
Staunch Irish Presbyterians; three-pointed sermons,
triangular sandwiches—keen on the Trinity.
To them, God lived among the rafters, not the pews,
and couldn't be this old man who, while watching the news,
would lift still-strong hands and start tapping a beat
on the arms of his chair while on the edge of his seat
he would whistle tunes that have carried different words
since the bandsmen picked up arms.
The God of Earth and Sky knew every hymn up, down

and across.
Nobody ever wrote him one.

At the service, we sang Abide With Me
and ate triangular sandwiches.
Afterwards, we climbed the hill we always used to,
opened the sweet tin and flung the contents skywards.
God made funeral confetti a real thing.
The youngest cousins had remote-controlled helicopters;
they chased the sky-bits up and up until
the batteries died, and they drifted back to earth
like God's last gifts.
It *was* Christmas.

When I get the chance I go home,
pull on God's old green wellies
and climb the hill, mud to my ankles.
There's a grave somewhere,
but if anything is sacred
it's this earth, not cold stone.
I drink tea with the hills, and tell the sky
the same jokes that he always did.
It doesn't usually laugh.
I'm probably not telling them right.
When it gets dark I descend,
vault the gate like Dad taught me
and head for the lights of home.
I pray, to the rain and the dirt,
that the pantheon is real.

Downhill

A
day
and a
half ago
I told you to
stand with me,
watch the sunrise,
pretend we snuck in
without buying tickets.
If all this life is a festival,
God's got an artist's pass.
He uses it for the free beers
and to get into the nicer loos.
Someone round here's got a gun
in their welly boot to keep the mud off.
Someone round here's got lost on purpose,
looking for God, the sky, some soup or a hug.
Not everyone has your sense of direction, old friend.
Please, please, throw me at yourself. Time flies. I don't.

clunk #4

I'd be remiss if I didn't remind you

to sea.
17 Perhaps the leopard can't change his
spots, but we can find the places which re-
member
18 the heat of this city as safari, pavements
baking under new eyes.

London, as a Cradle With Teeth

19 I am writing to you to tell you that my
reasons to fight have migrated West,
20 my body a new tomb refusing to roll
stones.
21 This city has raised us high enough to
burn in the sun, changing chicken shops for
the consolatory mouthfeel of ozone.
22 The men in my family wither in the
sunlight, but at the least their eyes are tilted
heavenwards;
23 I will not die in this city. LORD
willin'. LORD willin'.

Toes

The last time I stared into the abyss it filed a restraining order.
Sometimes strangers apologise to me for no reason;
perhaps I'm stepping on toes.
My earliest memory is realising that I had toes,
that human feet weren't, by nature or necessity, sock-shaped.
Mum and Dad had toes, too. Still do.
I find myself spending far too much time thinking
about the supermassive black hole
at the centre of our galaxy.
I wonder if it has toes.

clunk #5

Survived another winter(?)

Just Between Us

In a town I called 'home'
before I knew how
to say the word 'home'
there is a pub called
The Lighthouse.
I will need you
to take it on faith
that it is one.

I was born knowing
how to speak Human.
I forgot this the first time
I asked my mother,
"Am I a Hun or a Taig?
The boys at school
want to know."
She chased the world
from my shoulders
like a stray I brought in,
and said:
"I will need you
to take it on faith
that that is not a question
you should ever ask anyone."
At six, I couldn't see

over the sandbags,
but I understood,
and kept mum.

We unfold ourselves into
familiar seats with
familiar drinks.
I probe my wisdom teeth
for an unfamiliar word.
I let my brain slump across the table
as Ryan takes his shot.
I think of
centres and
spinning and
find, on my tongue,
the word 'Sanctuary' and
my phone vibrates.

Dad's hands have been
earthquaking since
they put the volcano
in his chest.
He works nights to keep
the lights on;
I find there's something
holy in that.

I have watched mountains
rise to meet his boots.

I have heard music
I could not hope to replicate
leap from his fingers.
I have seen the way he looks
when he thinks we're not.

I want to tell him:
"I will need you
to take it on faith
that you are not old
until I stop being
your little boy."
Instead, I make some joke:
"They'll have to rename it.
Parky never had chat like yours."

Autocorrect
speaks seismic.
"Get home safe."
I am.

We walk the same route.
Sea air: blanket.
Creating gods in the dark
from breath, shoulder touches
and every age I have ever been.
I leave tomorrow.
As we pass The Lighthouse,

I hear David Bowie
still asking if there's
Life on Mars.

I will need you
to take it on faith
that there's enough
life here
for both of us.

clunk #6

Pavement grumbles, railway, sleep.

```
[00:34] joel
[00:36] yes mate
[00:36] what sound does nostalgia
        make?
[00:37] like when you pull a horizon
        back, then let go?
[00:42] ok. and what kind of sound
        is that?
[00:43] a sort of dry boing, i think
[00:45] no. that's not right at all
[00:45] what do you mean?
[02:34] hello? are you still there?
[05:21] it's the sound of spinning
        plates.
```

Rucksack

Today I match pace with continents.
The drift of the world is soothing, still.
I don't appear in the photos I take;
my feet remember where they were.

The drift of the world is soothing. Still,
there are places I keep pressed and pinned.
My feet remember where they were:
3AM. Heel-turn. Door-click.

There are places I keep pressed and pinned.
You wear a rucksack when I next remember this.
3AM. Heel-turn. Door-click.
Sometimes the breeze has mountains in it.

You wear a rucksack. When I next remember this,
I don't appear. In the photos I take,
sometimes the breeze has mountains in it.
Today, I match pace with continents.

Acknowledgements

It would be very difficult to thank every single poet who has taught or influenced me—there are simply too many. Special thanks are in order, however, to Sarah Martin, Chris Lawrence, Bohdan Piasecki, Antosh Wojcik, Sara Hirsch, Caroline Teague, Tyrone Lewis, Aisling Fahey and Laurie Ogden.

Thanks also to Amy Acre and Jake Wild Hall of Bad Betty Press, the best publishers—and friends—I could have asked for.

To my parents, brothers and the rest of my family and friends for humouring and supporting my odd poetry habit—thanks for putting up with me.

Finally, and most importantly, to my late grandad Robert Bolton, who would have found the idea of being on the cover of a poetry book profoundly hilarious. And to my best friend Ally, who said he'd be sad if he didn't get a mention.

'Toes' was first published in *The Morning Star.*

The clunks (including an animated version of clunk 5) are published online at http://www.joelotter.com/clunks/

www.ingramcontent.com/pod-product-compliance
Ingram Content Group UK Ltd.
Pitfield, Milton Keynes, MK11 3LW, UK
UKHW062309290726
14090UKWH00018B/961